Creatures With Pockets

BY SUSAN HARRIS

Illustrated by Frankie Coventry

AN EASY-READ WILDLIFE BOOK
FRANKLIN WATTS
NEW YORK|LONDON|TORONTO|SYDNEY|1980

Contents

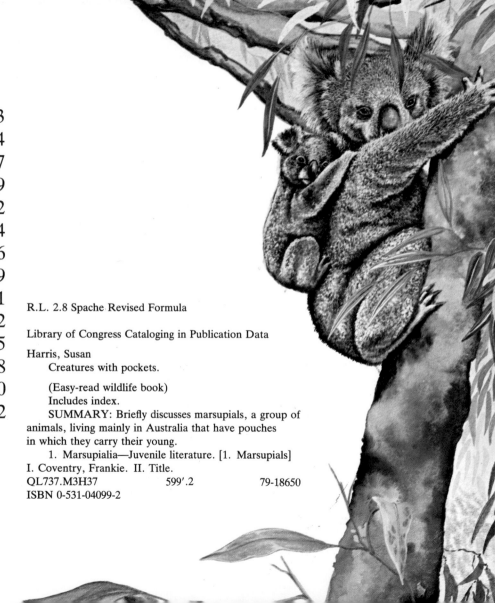

R.L. 2.8 Spache Revised Formula

Library of Congress Cataloging in Publication Data

Harris, Susan
    Creatures with pockets.

    (Easy-read wildlife book)
    Includes index.
    SUMMARY: Briefly discusses marsupials, a group of
animals, living mainly in Australia that have pouches
in which they carry their young.
    1. Marsupialia—Juvenile literature. [1. Marsupials]
I. Coventry, Frankie. II. Title.
QL737.M3H37   599′.2   79-18650
ISBN 0-531-04099-2

Introduction

After a dog gives birth to puppies, she usually stays close to them for a few weeks. While growing up, the puppies return to her when they need warmth or food.

There are some animals, though, that can carry their young with them all the time. They can do this because they have **pouches** or pockets. These animals are called **marsupials** (mar-SOO-pee-als). Most of them are found in Australia.

The name marsupial means "having a pouch." Only female marsupials have the pouch. They give birth to very small babies that are not yet completely developed. The babies are able to find their own way from the mother's birth canal to her pouch. There, they drink milk from the mother's **teats** (teets) or nipples, and grow bigger.

Kangaroo embryo in its mother's pouch

The Kangaroo

The **kangaroo** of Australia has the biggest pocket of all the pouched animals. Just before a baby kangaroo is born, the mother cleans out her pouch with her tongue.

When the baby is born, it is only about 1 inch (2.6 cm) long. Neither eyes nor ears have developed yet. Its hair has not yet grown in. With tiny but strong arms, it pulls itself into the pouch.

(Inset) **Actual size of young kangaroo embryo**

The baby grabs its mother's teat at once. It doesn't let go for many weeks. After about four months, it is strong enough to sit up and look out of the pouch.

Young kangaroos are known as **joeys**. Soon joey is able to jump out of the pouch to eat some grass.

If frightened, joey scampers quickly back to its mother. It dives back into the pouch, head first. Once inside, it turns a somersault to right itself.

5

For the first eight months of its life, joey spends much of its time in the pouch. It travels everywhere with its mother, sometimes at great speeds. Leaping, an adult kangaroo can go as fast as 20 miles (32 km) an hour.

After about eight months, joey is too large to fit into the pouch. Then it lives outside, eating grass just like a fully-grown kangaroo.

The Wallaby

The **wallaby** (WAL-a-bee) is another marsupial found in Australia. It is also found on the smaller islands that are nearby. It is a cousin of the kangaroo, and looks much like one. The main difference is that wallabies are smaller than kangaroos.

Like kangaroos, female wallabies have pouches for their young. They give birth to and raise their babies in much the same way as kangaroos.

And, like their kangaroo cousins, they often live in mobs of up to 20 individuals.

7

There are many different types of wallaby. One is called the pretty-face wallaby, named for its good looks. Another is the nail-tail wallaby. It has a horny growth, almost like a fingernail, at the tip of its tail. Swamp wallabies live in damp areas.

Rock wallabies live in rocky areas. They have special pads on their feet. These allow them to leap across rocks with great skill.

There is another type of kangaroo that is smaller than most kangaroos. But it is larger than most wallabies. It is called the **wallaroo** (WAL-a-roo)—a name that combines **walla**by and kanga**roo**.

The Koala

The **koala** (ko-A-la) is a marsupial with a different sort of pouch. Instead of opening on top, the pouch is "upside down." The baby koala looks at the world from between its mother's back legs.

You might think that the baby koala could fall out of its pouch. But it doesn't. There are special muscles around the opening of the pouch. These keep the baby safely inside.

Koalas are found in Australia. They live in **eucalyptus** (u-ka-LIP-tus), or gum, trees and feed on their leaves. They eat no other food and almost never drink water. In fact, they hardly ever come down from the trees.

10

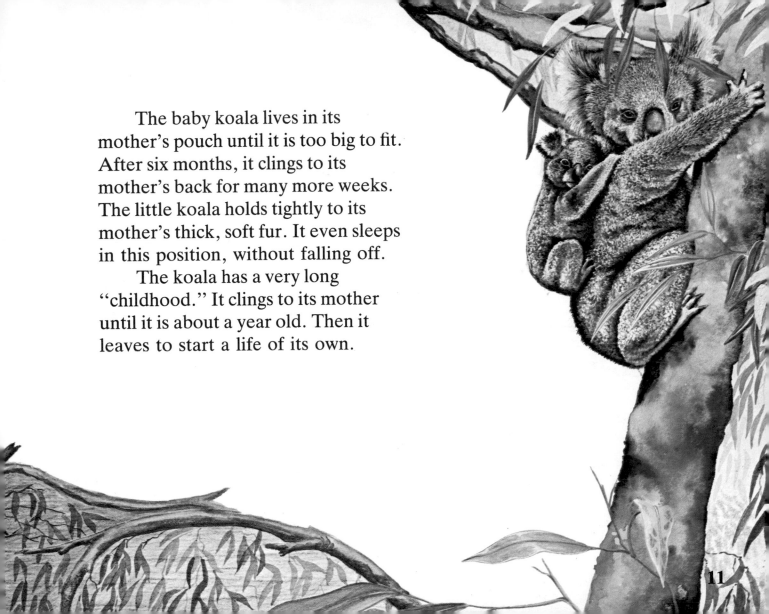

The baby koala lives in its
mother's pouch until it is too big to fit.
After six months, it clings to its
mother's back for many more weeks.
The little koala holds tightly to its
mother's thick, soft fur. It even sleeps
in this position, without falling off.

The koala has a very long
"childhood." It clings to its mother
until it is about a year old. Then it
leaves to start a life of its own.

The Bandicoot

Bandicoots (BAND-a-koots) are Australian marsupials about the size of rabbits.

Like the koala, the female's pouch opens at the back. The baby climbs in between the mother's back legs. This works out well for the young ones. The baby in the pouch is kept dirt-free when the mother scratches for insects.

The female bandicoot usually gives birth to two or three babies at a time.

12

They are tiny and hairless at birth. First, they find their way into the pouch. Then, they feed on their mother's milk for about five weeks.

At about ten weeks, they are too large to stay in the pouch. So they leave the pouch to live outside. But they still return and pop their heads in now and then to take a drink of milk.

The Tasmanian Devil

This strange dog-like animal also has a backwards-facing pouch.

The mother gives birth to three or four babies at a time. They live in her pouch until they are about ten weeks old. By this time, they are all too big for the pouch. So they hang outside. But they still hang from their mother's teats and drink her milk.

14

At about four months, they are able to eat solid food their mother brings them. Sometimes the mother will leave her young in a nest of leaves and twigs while she hunts for food.

She hunts only at night, and will eat possums, snakes, lizards, rabbits, wallabies, and birds.

The **Tasmanian** (tas-MANE-ee-an) **devil** is about the size of a small dog. It is found only on the island of **Tasmania**, south of Australia.

They actually look devilish with their black hair and sharp teeth. But in fact, they are quite harmless to people.

The Possum

In Australia, there are
many different kinds of
possum. Long ago, they
were named **"opossums"**
(o-POS-sums) by the
explorer Captain Cook. He
thought they looked much
like the opossums of
America. But Australians
dropped the "o" and they
are now known as possums.

Possums live in trees and bush areas. The brush-tailed possum even lives in suburbs and towns in Australia. They are usually very tame, as long as they are not disturbed. Some people even keep them as pets.

The brush-tailed possum is about the size of a cat. The female has a layer of skin on her **abdomen** (AB-do-men) which forms a pouch.

Normally one, but sometimes two babies are born each year. It lives on its mother's milk for about four months. Then it is strong enough to climb onto its mother's back. For the next few months, she will carry it "piggyback" wherever she goes. Later it will crawl along the branches on its own.

The Pouched Mouse

There is even a mouse-like marsupial in Australia with a pouch. The female gives birth to six or seven babies at one time. Her pouch is small, and she can't hold them all.

So, the ones that can't fit hold on outside her pouch. But they drink her milk until they are old enough to feed themselves.

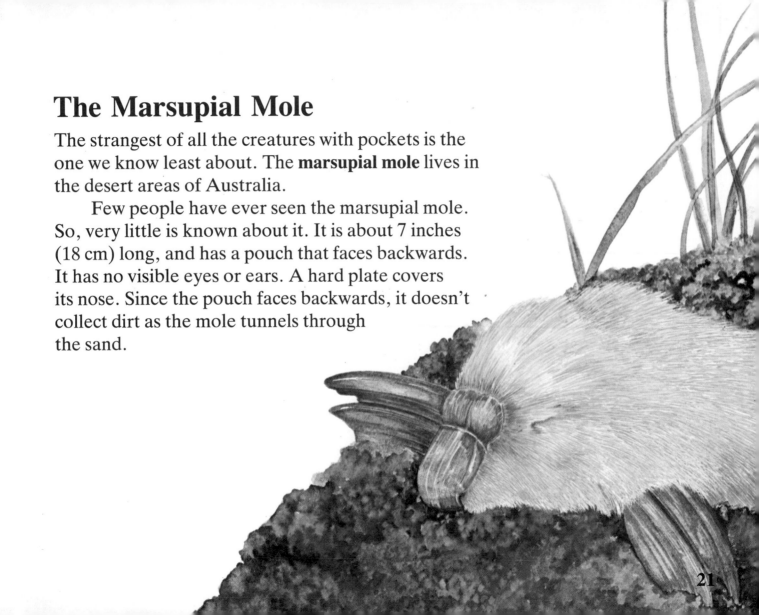

The Marsupial Mole

The strangest of all the creatures with pockets is the one we know least about. The **marsupial mole** lives in the desert areas of Australia.

Few people have ever seen the marsupial mole. So, very little is known about it. It is about 7 inches (18 cm) long, and has a pouch that faces backwards. It has no visible eyes or ears. A hard plate covers its nose. Since the pouch faces backwards, it doesn't collect dirt as the mole tunnels through the sand.

The Wombat

Another Australian animal with a pocket is the **wombat**. Its pocket faces backwards. Wombats grow to be about 36 inches (90 cm) long. They have dark brown or black fur.

The wombat is a burrower.
It digs its home with its
powerful front paws and claws.
It is therefore important that
the baby faces backwards.
Otherwise, it would be hit with
dirt and stones as its mother
digs her burrow.

Wombats build long, wide tunnels. They live in these burrows in the daytime. At night, they come out to feed on grass, roots, and bark.

Wombats have strong, sharp teeth and sharp curved claws. But they are really quite harmless. In fact, some people keep them as pets.

When a young wombat is about six months old, it leaves the pouch for good. Later, it goes off to make a life of its own.

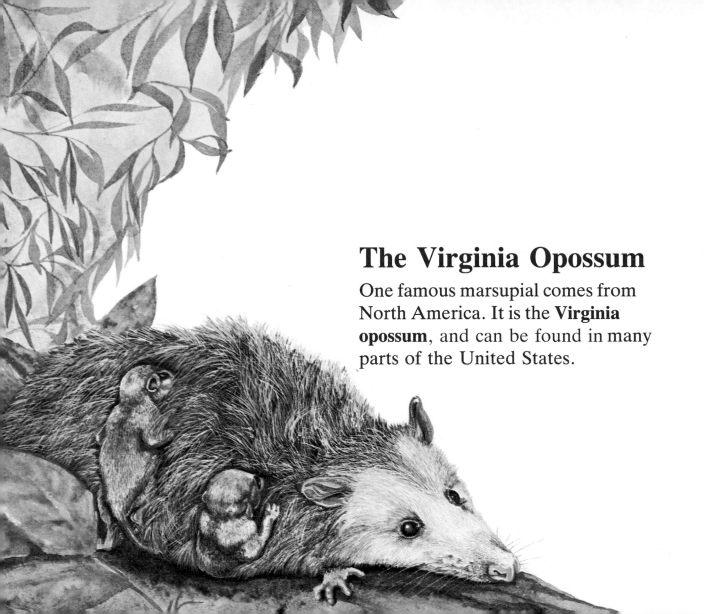

The Virginia Opossum

One famous marsupial comes from North America. It is the **Virginia opossum**, and can be found in many parts of the United States.

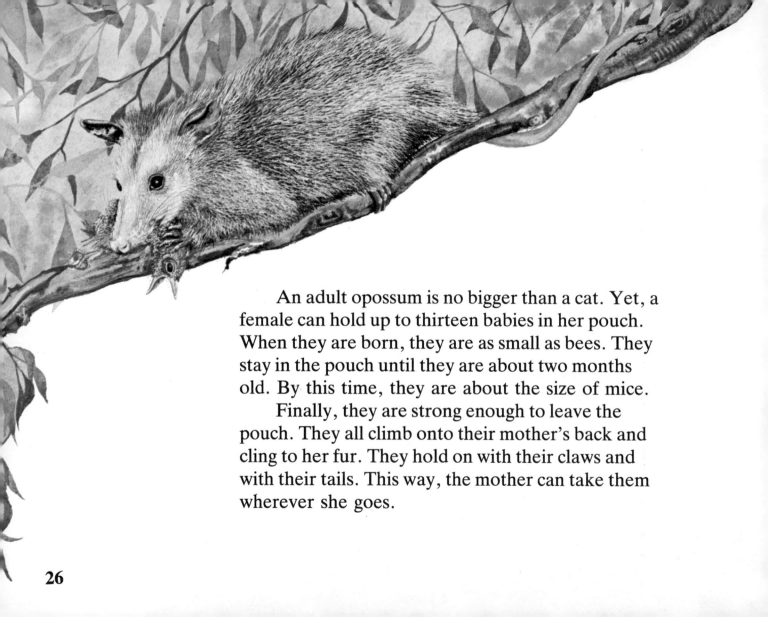

An adult opossum is no bigger than a cat. Yet, a female can hold up to thirteen babies in her pouch. When they are born, they are as small as bees. They stay in the pouch until they are about two months old. By this time, they are about the size of mice.

Finally, they are strong enough to leave the pouch. They all climb onto their mother's back and cling to her fur. They hold on with their claws and with their tails. This way, the mother can take them wherever she goes.

The mother takes her young with her as she looks for food at night. Opossums like to eat birds, fruit, eggs, and insects.

While climbing trees, she can curl her long tail around branches to steady herself. This type of gripping tail is known as a **prehensile** (pre-HEN-sil) tail.

27

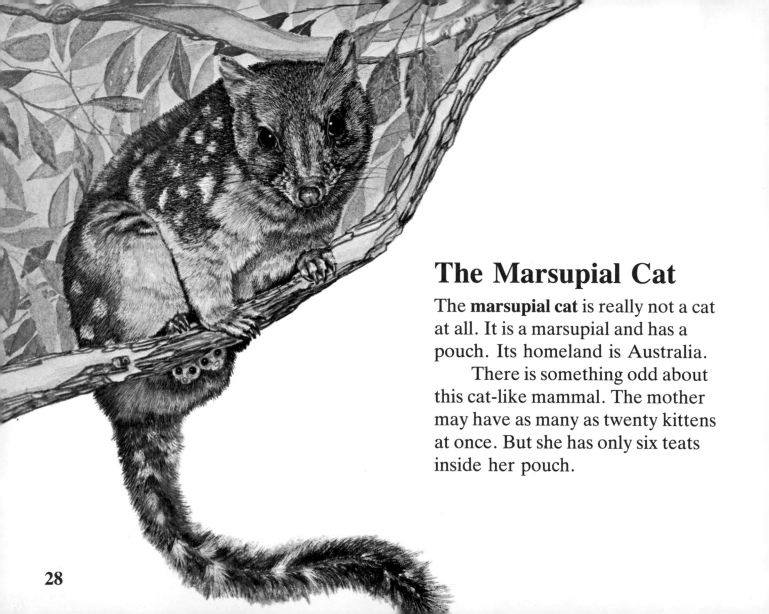

The Marsupial Cat

The **marsupial cat** is really not a cat at all. It is a marsupial and has a pouch. Its homeland is Australia.

There is something odd about this cat-like mammal. The mother may have as many as twenty kittens at once. But she has only six teats inside her pouch.

So, the first six kittens that reach the milk supply will live. All the others die.

Those that do live are able to leave the pouch at about five months.

The marsupial cat lives in hollow logs or dead trees. It eats mice, rats, lizards, and large insects.

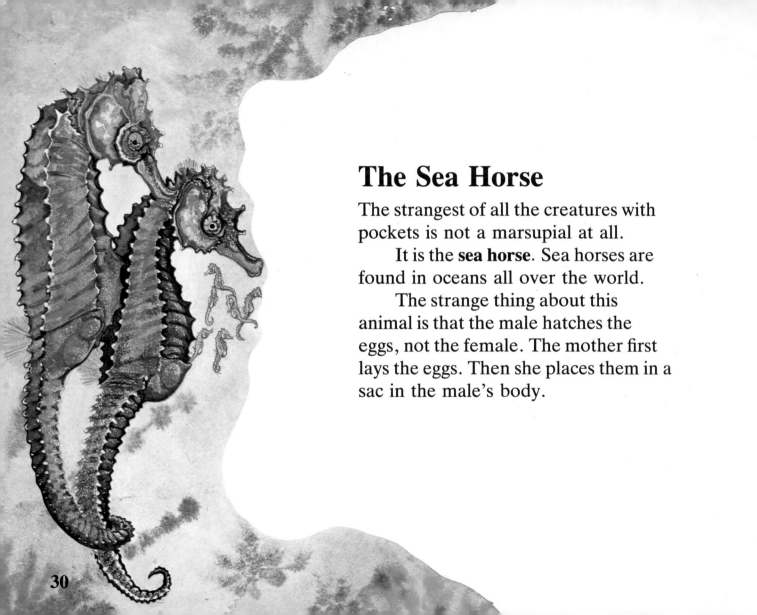

The Sea Horse

The strangest of all the creatures with pockets is not a marsupial at all.

It is the **sea horse**. Sea horses are found in oceans all over the world.

The strange thing about this animal is that the male hatches the eggs, not the female. The mother first lays the eggs. Then she places them in a sac in the male's body.

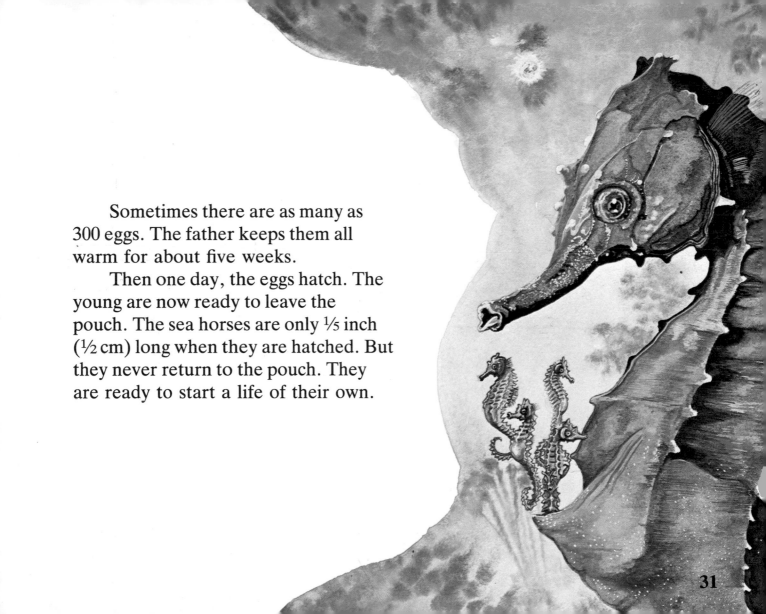

Sometimes there are as many as 300 eggs. The father keeps them all warm for about five weeks.

Then one day, the eggs hatch. The young are now ready to leave the pouch. The sea horses are only ⅕ inch (½ cm) long when they are hatched. But they never return to the pouch. They are ready to start a life of their own.

Index